HAVE A positive IMPACT... ...ON Society

by John Wood

KidHaven PUBLISHING

Published in 2025 by
KidHaven Publishing, an Imprint of
Greenhaven Publishing, LLC
2544 Clinton St., Buffalo, NY 14224

Written by: John Wood
Edited by: Rebecca Phillips-Bartlett
Designed by: Amelia Harris

All facts, statistics, web addresses and URLs in this book were verified as valid and accurate at time of writing. No responsibility for any changes to external websites or references can be accepted by either the author or publisher.

Cataloging-in-Publication Data

Names: Wood, John, 1990-.
Title: On society / John Wood.
Description: Buffalo, New York : KidHaven Publishing, 2025. | Series: Have a positive impact… | Includes glossary and index.
Identifiers: ISBN 9781534547520 (pbk.) | ISBN 9781534547537 (library bound) | ISBN 9781534547544 (ebook)
Subjects: LCSH: Empathy--Juvenile literature. | Happiness--Juvenile literature. | Self-esteem--Juvenile literature.
Classification: LCC BF575.E55 W66 2025 | DDC 155.4'1241--dc23

Manufactured in the United States of America

CPSIA compliance information: Batch #CSKH25
For further information contact Greenhaven Publishing LLC at 1-844-317-7404.

Please visit our website, www.greenhavenpublishing.com.
For a free color catalog of all our high-quality books, call toll free 1-844-317-7404 or fax 1-844-317-7405.

Find us on

Contents

Words that look like <u>this</u> are explained in the glossary on page 31.

Your Place

You belong to lots of different groups. You might belong to a sports team, a class at school, or a club outside of school. You belong to a family, too. Family groups can be all sorts of shapes and sizes.

Belonging to a group is important. Being together can make us feel better. Together we can help each other do things we wouldn't be able to do alone. It's much easier to have a positive impact when you have your friends and family around you.

When you belong to a group, it means that you are an important part of it. You will often have certain things you must do. As a student, you are an important part of your school and you have a very important job – learning!

Students learn at home, too.

But did you know you are part of something else, too? You are part of something much bigger than families, schools, clubs, and teams. You are part of society.

What Is Society?

Society can mean different things, but usually it is a word for a big group of people who follow the same rules and share resources. A society can be a whole country of people, or people from more than one country together. In a society, we make sure that nobody is alone or unsafe.

BEING PART OF SOCIETY IS ONE WAY THAT WE LOOK AFTER EACH OTHER.

People don't have to live near each other, speak the same language, or think the same things to be part of a society. This means society is full of lots of different types of people. Everybody in a society should be treated fairly and equally.

Ancient Egypt

Ancient Egypt was a society. It was mostly made up of villages near the River Nile. The farmers living in the villages had very different lives than the pharaoh, who ruled in the capital. However, they all belonged to the same society, and everyone had an important part to play.

Ancient Egyptian society lasted for around 3,000 years.

The United States

The United States is a big country made up of 50 states. Each state is different, and traveling between them can sometimes feel like going to different countries! However, the people in each state all belong to the same society.

This valley is in the U.S. state of Arizona...

...and this town is in another U.S. state, Vermont.

Being a Member of Society

When you are part of society, it is called being a member of society. It can also be called being a citizen when you are part of a country. Society works best when the members do good things for each other. This is called contributing to society.

Everybody contributes to society in their own way. The most important thing is to treat others with kindness and respect.

In a good society, people look after the planet, too.

What Do Citizens Do?

Adult citizens often do certain things to contribute to society. For example, they pay money to the government. These payments are called taxes. Adults also vote on who should be part of the government to lead society.

People vote in elections. Elections usually happen every few years. It is different in different countries.

You don't have to do any of those things right now. At the moment, your role in society is to grow and learn. However, there are things that you can do today to make a difference and be a good citizen.

Social Awareness

The first step to making society a better place is to grow your social awareness. This means being aware of how other people feel.

Social Awareness in Action

Imagine there is a new student at your school. At lunch, they sit on their own. They are quiet and they are always looking down at their lunch. How might they feel? Could they be scared or nervous? Maybe they are not confident enough to join in. Using social awareness, you could help and invite them to your table.

How to Grow Social Awareness

A society where we are aware of each others' feelings will be stronger, fairer, and better. The best way to grow your social awareness is to listen to other people's stories and their opinions. Find out how they see the world and what matters to them. Make sure you listen to all sorts of people – not just people who are like you.

People put their stories, feelings, and opinions in books, films, and songs, too. So read, watch, and listen to grow your social awareness even more!

THINK ABOUT OTHERS AND THEIR FEELINGS BEFORE YOU SPEAK OR ACT.

Social Progress

Society can always get better. As each citizen makes a positive impact, life can improve for everyone, bit by bit. In many ways, most societies today are much fairer for everyone than societies in history.

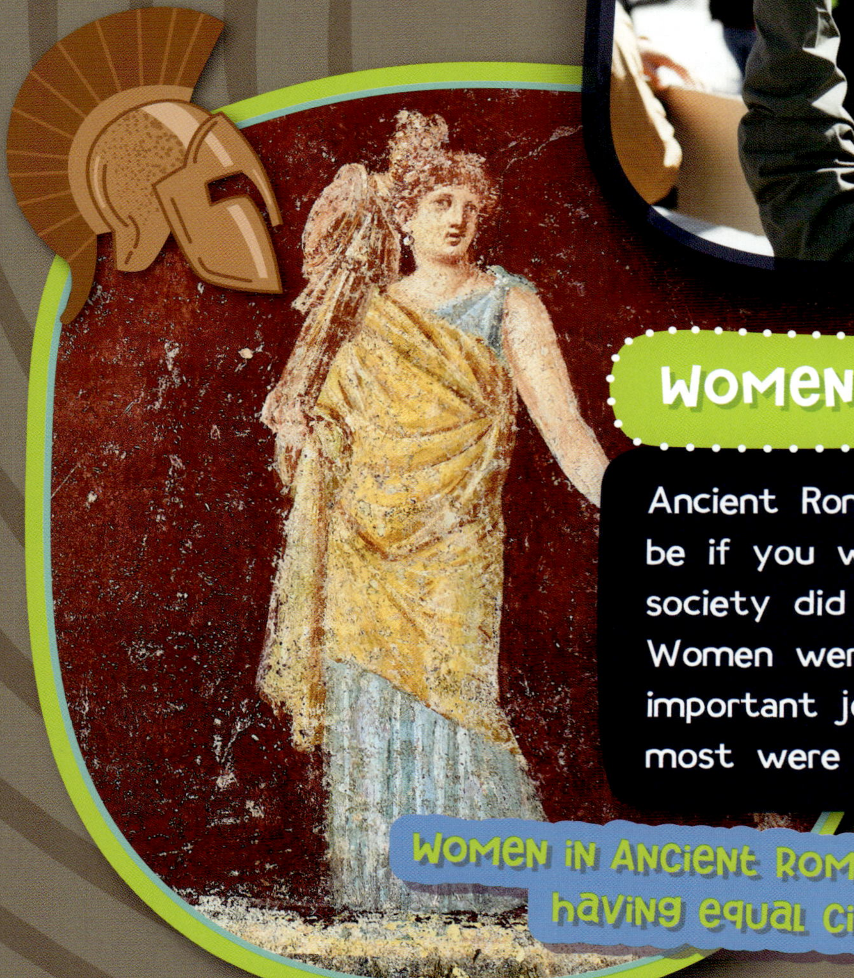

Women in Roman Times

Ancient Rome was a horrible place to be if you were a woman. The men in society did not treat women fairly. Women were not allowed to have important jobs, they couldn´t vote. and most were not taught to read or write.

Women in Ancient Rome were not considered as having equal citizenship with men.

In many societies today, everyone agrees that women are equal to men. Today, many women around the world have more rights than they did during Roman times. It has taken a long time to make society fairer for women, but it shows that society can get better, even if it takes many, many years.

Suffragettes, San Francisco, U.S., 1915

These women, and many others like them, changed people's minds about making society fairer for women.

There is still more work to do in order to make society fairer and better for everyone. Turn to the next page for some ideas of what you can do to have a positive impact.

Small Things

Saying and Doing

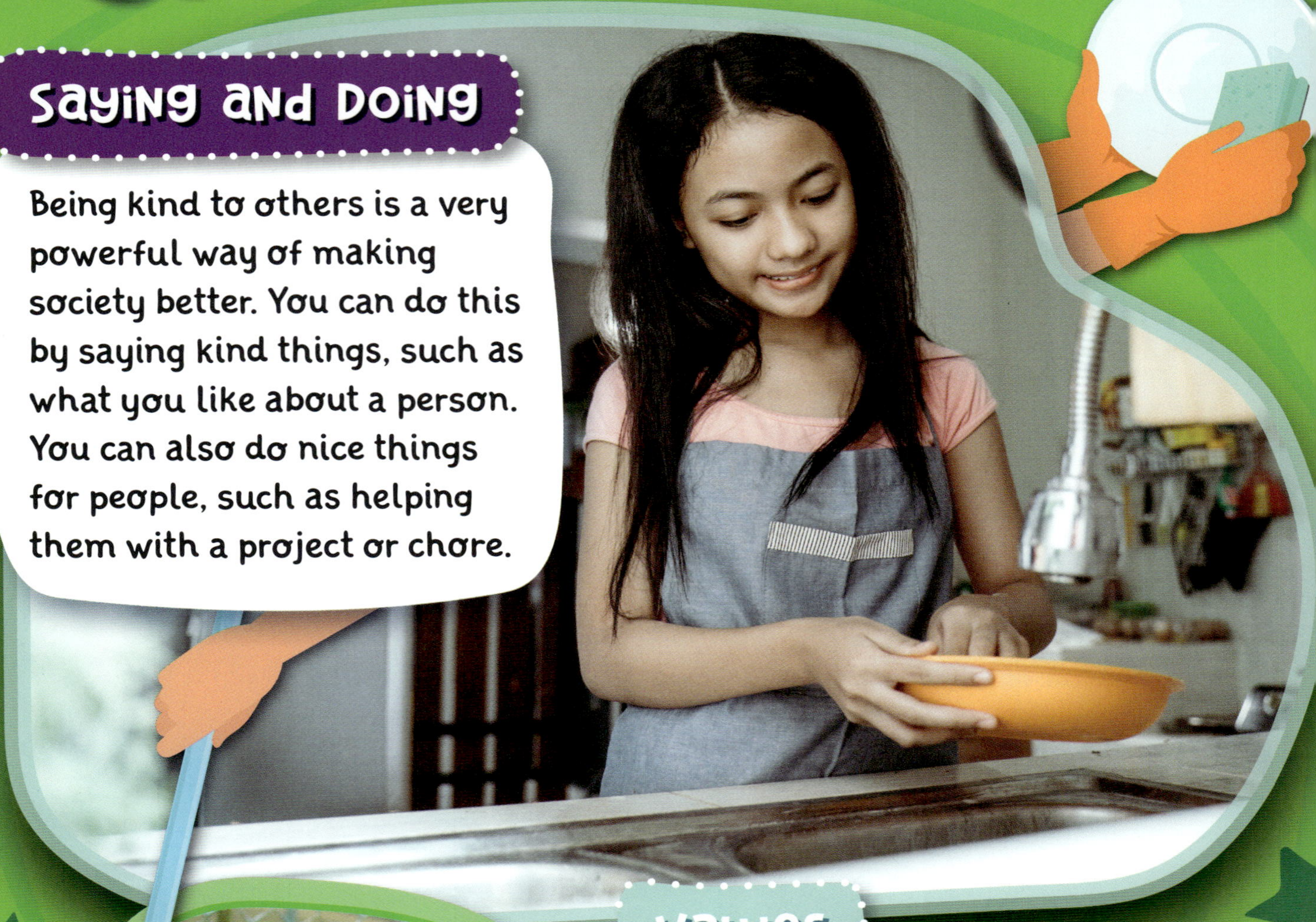

Being kind to others is a very powerful way of making society better. You can do this by saying kind things, such as what you like about a person. You can also do nice things for people, such as helping them with a project or chore.

Values

Every society has values that are important. Values are ways of living that most people agree are good and should be a part of everyday life. For example, many societies value respect. Societies might also value things such as freedom, fairness, and looking after the planet.

WHAT ARE YOUR VALUES?

No Discrimination

When someone judges a person before they get to know them, it is called prejudice. Prejudice is bad because people might be treated unfairly because of how they look or where they come from, instead of who they are – this is called discrimination. Many societies believe it isn't right to discriminate against others. You can uphold this value by not forming an opinion on someone before you get to know them.

Equality

Many societies believe in equality, meaning everybody is equal and treated fairly. You can uphold this value by making sure everyone is included and has a turn in games, sports, and activities.

Volunteering

Volunteering means giving up your time to help others. People do not get anything in return for volunteering. They do it because they believe it is important and the right thing to do. Volunteering can have a big positive impact on society.

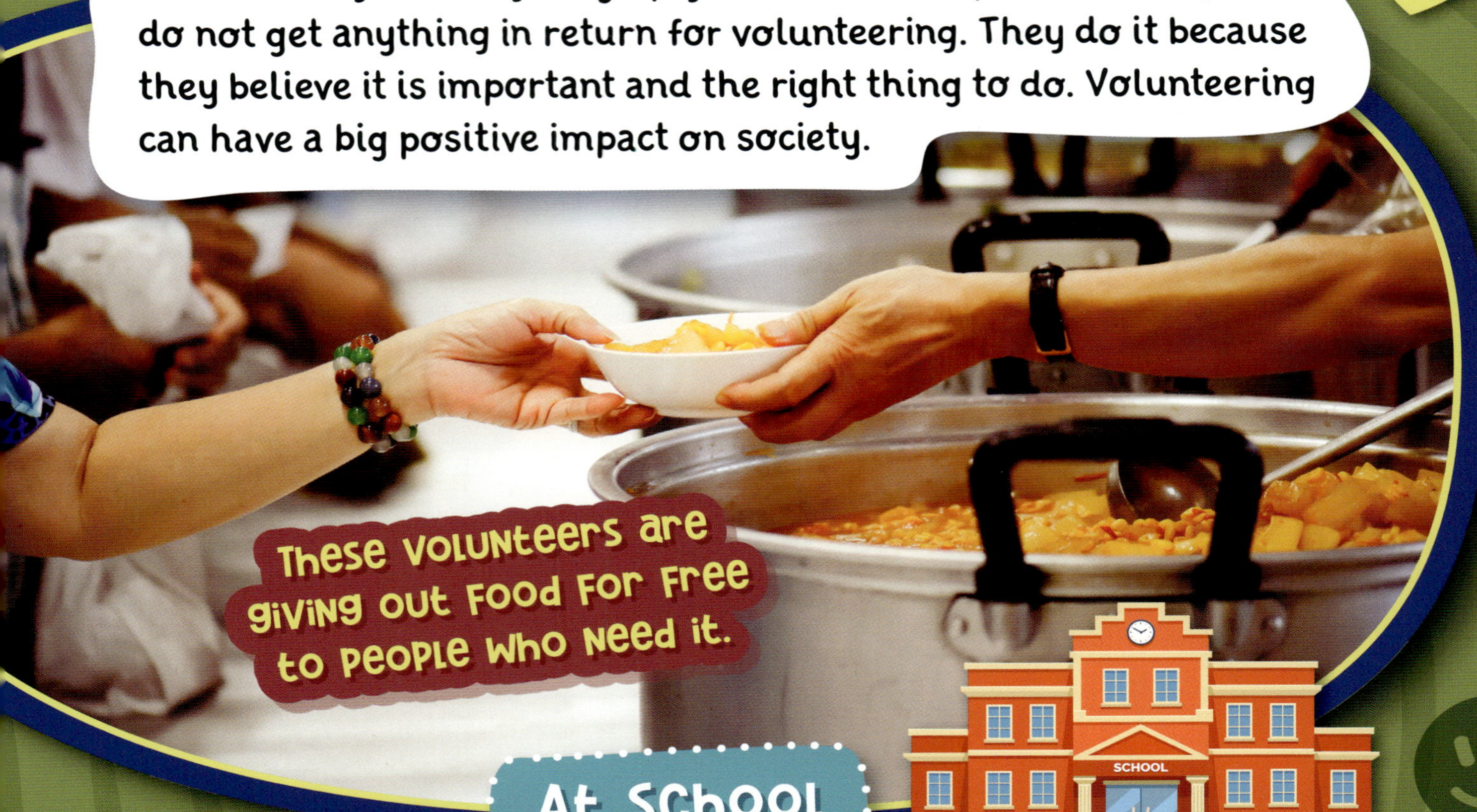

These volunteers are giving out food for free to people who need it.

At School

You could have a positive impact at school by volunteering. You could ask a teacher if you can help younger children with their reading. You could also help teachers set up and prepare for after-school clubs and activities.

Residential Homes

A residential home is where some people go to live when they are older. You could volunteer by visiting a residential home with your school or family. Make friends with the people who live there. You could set up activities for people to do or perform a song to entertain them.

Parks

Another way to volunteer is picking up litter at a park. Not only does this make the area nicer for everyone who lives nearby, but it also helps the animals and plants. Ask your friends and family to volunteer with you.

Volunteering is more fun together.

Standing Up FOR What You Believe In

You can change society for the better by being an activist. An activist is someone who tells people about important issues and tries to change people's minds. There are many ways to do this.

These activists are telling people about the importance of climate change.

Marches and Protests

In a protest, people stand on the street or outside a building to talk about something important. They often have signs and banners, and they might chant or shout together so everybody is aware of the issue. A march is similar, but people walk the streets instead.

This is a Pride march. Pride is about people being free to love, marry, and be whoever they want.

CONSUMER ACTIVISM

Some activists change society by being careful about which companies they buy from. Ask your adults if they can choose companies that have good values, or companies that give money to charity.

BE KIND ONLINE

You can have a positive impact by being kind to others online. Leave kind comments and speak to others with respect. You can also report and block people who are being mean to others.

It is easy to forget that we are talking to real people online, who have real feelings and will be upset if others are rude.

Places in the Community

A good society has many community spaces. These are places where people can meet, talk, and help each other. Here are some examples of community spaces:

Community centers

Places of worship, such as churches and mosques

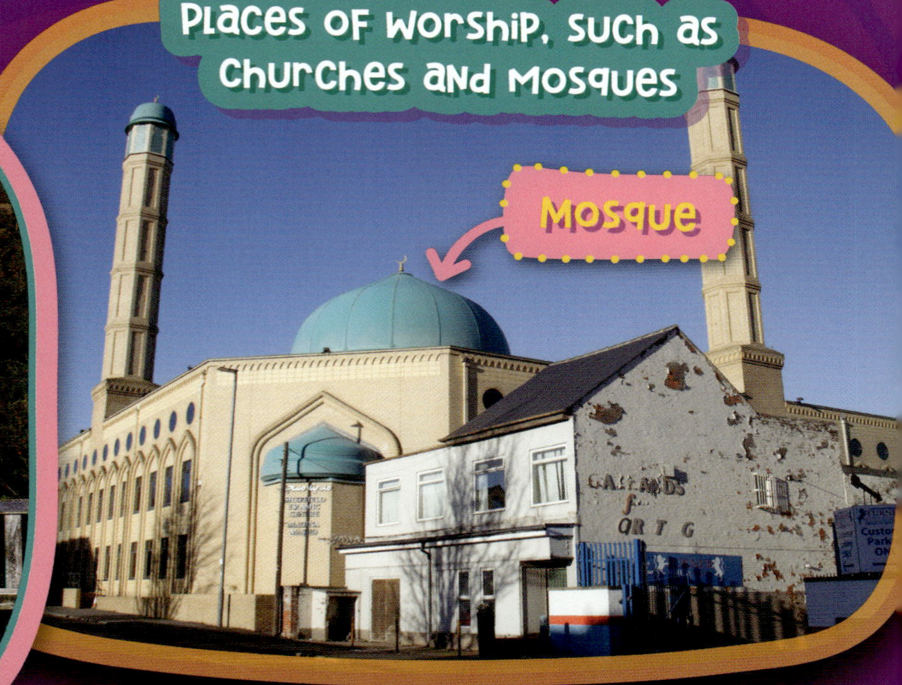

Art centers, such as theaters or art galleries

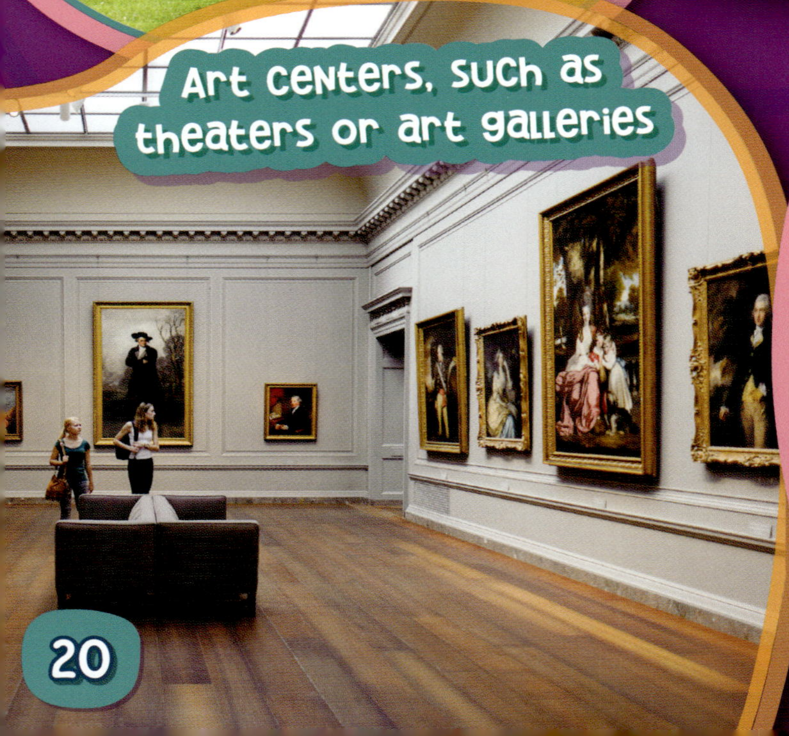

Sports centers and stadiums

Joining the Community

If there are no community spaces, people may not care as much about society and everyone around them. You can make a difference to society and yourself by joining a community space and going every week or every month. You might really enjoy it!

Once you have joined, you can ask if there is anything you can do to help. You might be able to volunteer and help run activities or keep the place neat and tidy. Thanks to you, the community space might grow and grow!

Politics

Politics means things dealing with the government and deciding how to run the country. The government decides the rules and <u>laws</u> that every person has to follow. It is a very important part of society.

In the U.S., the government meets and works in the U.S. Capitol.

Many societies vote for who gets to lead a country. Every adult gets one vote each election, and they vote for the <u>political party</u> they most agree with. This can be a fair way of deciding the rules.

Each person's vote is done in secret.

How Can Politics Help with Society?

Politics helps decide how the government can improve society. For example, will they build more houses, schools, and hospitals? What will be taught in schools? How much money will be spent on repairing roads and helping people who are less fortunate or too sick to work?

When you grow up, make sure you vote!

How Can You Help with Politics?

You can help make society better through politics. You can write a letter to the government and tell them what needs to change. You can also sign a petition. A petition is a document that asks the government to change something. In many countries, if enough people sign a petition, then the government has to look at it.

You can sign petitions online, too.

Art

Art doesn't just mean paintings. Art can be many things, such as dance, music, poetry, plays, and books. These things are important because they can entertain us and make us feel emotions, such as happiness.

This room full of giant chairs and tables is art!

Art can also be used to tell stories. It can help us understand people in society. For example, someone could write a song about what it is like for them to live in society, or write a book about the problems they face in society.

Art in Society

Art can change and improve society. Try making art for society yourself. You could use chalk on the pavement to draw pictures or write nice messages to other citizens. You could also hang pictures outside your home for people on the street to see. Just make sure you don't accidentally damage anything with your art!

Some people put on plays or play music outside for other members of society.

Some communities have little libraries in small spaces, such as a fun book box in someone's yard. If this exists near you, donate some books. If not, ask an adult to help you set one up.

BE THE CHANGE YOU WANT TO SEE IN SOCIETY.

Jobs That Help Society

Many jobs help society, but here are some that can have a big positive impact.

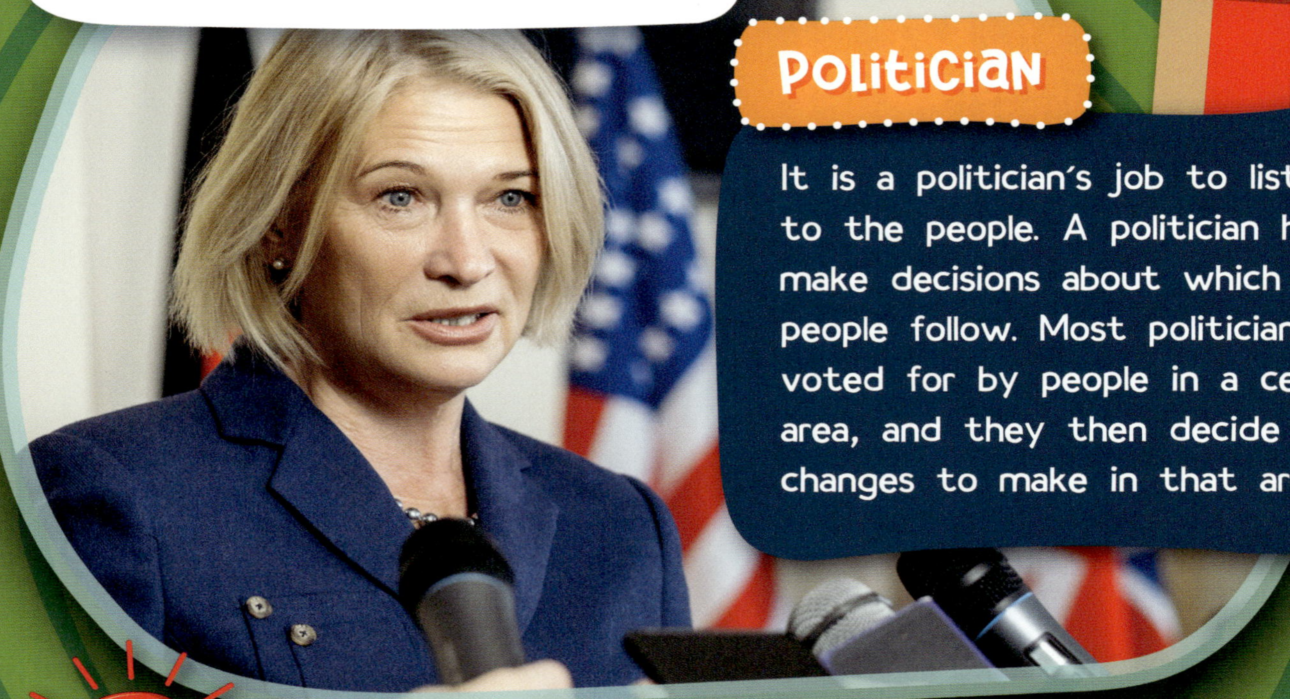

Politician

It is a politician's job to listen to the people. A politician helps make decisions about which laws people follow. Most politicians are voted for by people in a certain area, and they then decide what changes to make in that area.

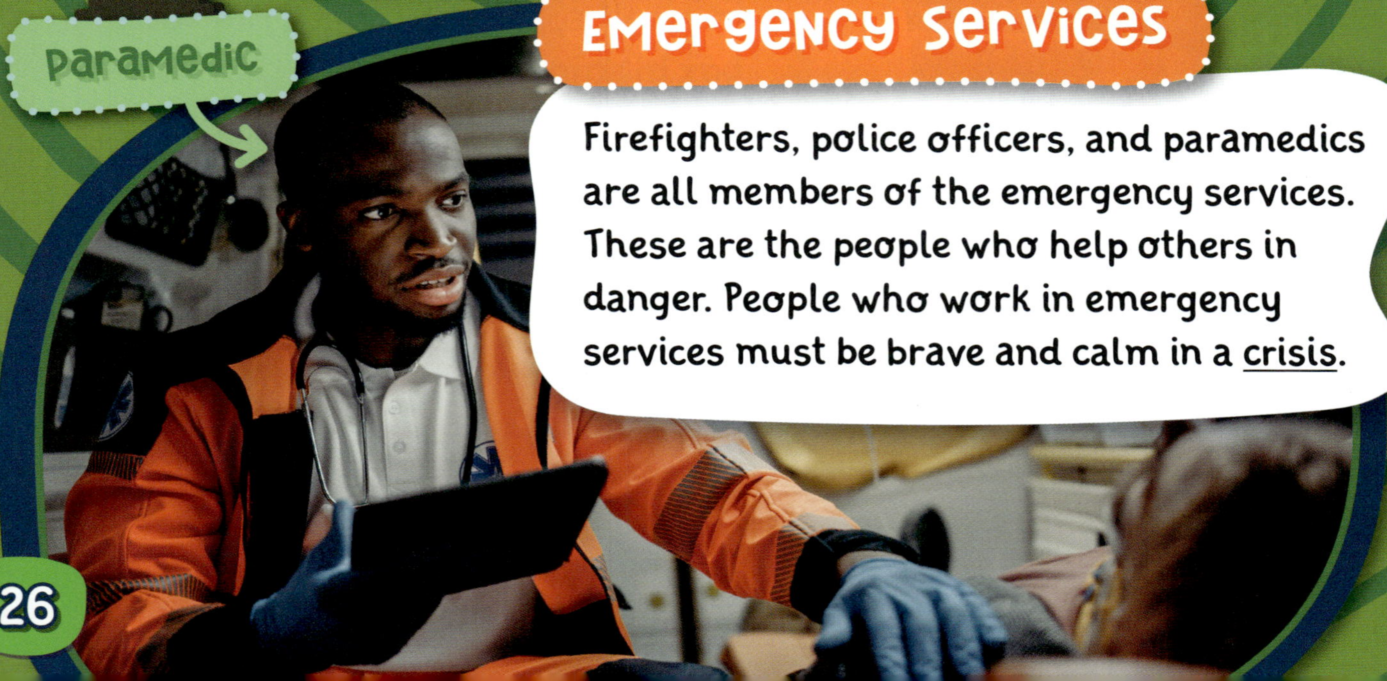

Emergency Services

Firefighters, police officers, and paramedics are all members of the emergency services. These are the people who help others in danger. People who work in emergency services must be brave and calm in a crisis.

Social Worker

Social workers protect vulnerable people from harm. They talk with all sorts of people and help to solve their problems. The most important skills for being a good social worker are listening and helping other people.

Scientist

Scientists are smart and curious. They try to understand how our world works. The things they discover can be amazing for society. Scientists do research and make discoveries that can lead to new medicines, new technology, new sources of energy. and more.

Teacher

One of the most important jobs is teaching. Teachers are often clever, patient, and good leaders. They are responsible for training the next generation to grow up to look after the world. Some teachers work in schools, while others work in universities.

Trash Collector

The people who take your trash away are called trash collectors. Society cannot exist without important jobs such as trash collectors. They work hard, driving across cities, towns, and villages in trucks to collect garbage and recycling.

Engineer

Engineers solve problems in the real world using science and math. For example, they build bridges, design new parts for spacecraft, figure out how to build new systems for cleaning water, and much more.

Librarian

Libraries are places where people go to understand the world. In a library, everyone can learn for free using books and computers. These are important places for the community, which makes librarians important people. Librarians are good at helping people and helping society.

Society AND You

Society is a busy place, and it is always changing. But there are two things that are always true — you belong here and you can make a difference. It is up to you to decide what difference you want to make!

What do you want to see in the world? If you could change anything, what would you change? It can be big or it can be small – it is up to you!

Glossary

capital	an important city or town where the government is based
climate change	a change in the typical weather or temperature of a large area
community centers	places where people from the community can go and take part in activities together
crisis	a dangerous or difficult time
document	a piece of paper or a file on a computer that has information in it
generation	a group of people who are about the same age
government	the group of people with the power to run a country and decide its laws
issues	important problems
judges	has an opinion about something or someone
laws	rules that a group of people must follow
political party	an organized group of people who have shared beliefs about how the country should be run
resources	supplies of money, materials, or people
respect	thinking good things about (or looking up to) someone or something
rights	sometimes called human rights, the things that every person deserves to have, such as the right to be free or the right to education
states	areas of a country that are separate but share the same government

Index

Image Credits

All images are courtesy of Shutterstock.com, unless otherwise specified. With thanks to Getty Images, Thinkstock Photo and iStockphoto. Recurring images – imagewriter. Cover – Fotokostic, Alonafoto, Tsapui, New Africa, WIROJE PATHI. 2–3 – Varavin88. 4–5 – Monkey Business Images, PeopleImages.com – Yuri A, HappyPictures, fizkes, Mind Pixell, Angelina Bambina, blvdone, irin-k. 6–7 – NicoElNino, melitas, Nuva Frames, hemro, Lucky-photographer, NEKVT, Simply Amazing, Anna Shalygina. 8–9 – Iryna Inshyna, Guppic the duck, PRASANNAPIX, Alistair McLellan, Buravleva stock, Jacob Lund, Amanita Silvicora. 10–11 – SeventyFour, LightField Studios, BRO.vector, Africa Studio, JR-50, Tartila, Pixel-Shot. 12–13 – Ground Picture, BlackMac, Sensvector, Everett Collection, Kitreel, Mary Long, Dotidrop. 14–15 – Odua Images, Tania Kolinko, NotionPic, oneinchpunch, matimix, RNko7. 16–17 – addkm, danielholmhansen, WinWinFolly, Granate Art, anetta, Stock-Asso, airdone, Tarzhanova. 18–19 – Holli, Kirkam, Irina Strelnikova, Miller Inna, sirtravelalot, Jesse33, Tymofeys, Jemastock, BRO.vector. 20–21 – Ben Molyneux, Duncan Andison, Vereshchagin Dmitry, Anton_Ivanov, chingyunsong, Daisy Daisy, inspiring.team, SrideeStudio. 22–23 – maziarz, Nancy Beijersbergen, Mascha Tace, Peeradach R, pics five, mentalmind, Lisa F. Young, GERARD BOTTINO, Menara Grafis. 24–25 – lev radin, criben, Look_Studio, lemono, Bibadash, Karlo Curis, Joe Dunckley, marishkaSm, New Africa, BRO.vector. 26–27 – Pressmaster, Gorodenkoff, graficriver_icons_logo, NotionPic, DGLimages. 28–29 – Monkey Business Images, Dmitry Kalinovsky, GoodStudio, Bullstar, stockphoto-graf. 30–31 – Gorodenkoff, jamesteohart, Irina Strelnikova.